Purposeful Poetry

JUSTIN WIDENER

ISBN 978-1-956001-33-4 (paperback)
ISBN 978-1-956001-34-1 (eBook)

Copyright © 2021 by Justin Widener

All rights reserved. No part of this publication may be reproduced, distributed, or transmitted in any form or by any means, including photocopying, recording, or other electronic or mechanical methods without the prior written permission of the publisher.

Printed in the United States of America

A Fairy Tale Life

A fairy tale life with love that has no end
Two little children and a house built with a fence
Princess or a Prince is what you dream of
A wedding in a church with unconditional love

Then one day you awake before your eyes you find
Your life is not that way and dreams are left behind
Your life is full of chaos the walls are coming down
The earth your feet are one is now a shaking ground

A lie is being whispered through your open ear
Your life is not over neither is the end near
In God your life remains and Christ is the start
Quit listening with your mind and listen with your heart

What's broken God will fix He will make it whole
He knows what's in your heart and carry in your soul
Don't question what he's done it is not a mistake
Your partner in this life a bond that He did make

Do not live your life according to all man
Turn your eyes to the king and with you He will stand
Come weather or the winds that want to just destroy
Standing in the Lord you'll live in lasting joy

So dream of what is best and what he wants for you
And pray for one another as they pray for you too
Keep your hope in Christ and build up all the faith
Trusting that His plan will guide you everyday

A Humble Life

Some people want the largest of homes
To spend the most money on sushi and scones
Several cars in the drive a motorcycle too
They will never been happy with less than a few

With clothes all the many and shoes a galore
They keep spending money to get so much more
They try to buy love and pay for some peace
They spoil their children nephew and niece

God spoke of these people who lose track of life
They've lost out on family their job and their wife
The days that fly by with very little joy
No time to throw a ball to that once little boy

There is still some time for them to have hope
Just change of your ways before you are broke
Materials are lost over time they are gone
But lessen your stress you just can't go wrong

Turn to the man who died on the cross
Let go of the world and all of the loss
You can find all the peace no pain or the strife
Know you are loved and live a humble life

A Pool

No wave in site or ripple alike
The boat is steady and weather is right
Some clouds do sit in the distant sky
The birds will circle and fly on by

A breeze blows gentle upon my face
Just me and my Lord here in this place
The wind blows harder out of the south
The clouds grow dark and rains pours out

This storm is strong with lightning above
No thing I shall fear I'm found in His love
The boat is being rocked come to and fro
What does my fate hold He only knows

This pain that I feel within my heart
Consuming my days when does the peace start
Tossed all about my body is worn
Please help me Lord my sails have torn

His presence is real He will hold us close
He gives us his strength our heart finally knows
The clouds are all gone by my side where he stands
This is just a pool trust in Him is the plan

A Process

An old man moans
And moves real slow
His bones they hurt
Every step he'll go

Will I die
Here in this place
Will I receive
Any mercy or grace

As a potter begins
With a little ball of clay
He works and molds
In a miraculous way

But the clay gets dry
And hard for the potter
To bring back life
He will use just water

The water gives life
Helps old become new
Makes the muscles of old
To stretch and to move

(continued on next page)

PURPOSEFUL POETRY

God is our potter
The one who controls
Release all the fear
To the hands that will hold

Fill your body with the spirit
And stand firm in belief
Just trust in our God
And feel the relief

We are all a process
God's work is not done
God will create beauty
In all not just some

A Puzzle

The pieces are small and come in a box
Some with curved edges that fit in a lock
Easy to find or easy to lose
The picture I see doesn't look like a moose

Where do I start which piece will come next
Piece with the face or the piece with the text
They sit in a pile right here before me
Just as my life like a wreck with debris

I pray to you God ask for help with this mess
Lessen this load find a way from this stress
Look down at the pieces take a look at my life
Find the reason I'm here with my children and wife

Come back to the pile and see something new
The piece that comes next a much better view
I trust in you Lord for the direction I must go
To follow your word your guidance will show

It starts to connect the pieces to the other
Just like a family with a sister and a brother
The picture is showing I start to understand
The walk with you Lord while you hold my hand

The puzzle complete the beauty it shows
Your radiant love the light that it glows
Control of my life I give unto you
I'll follow you Lord enjoying the view

American Soldiers

When you were young you hope to be
A Marine, sailor, airman or in the Army
You practiced your march and how you should stand
You tried to be stealthy and blend in with the land

As time would go by the chance would come near
With no hesitation your name is signed here
You have pride in your heart and love of country
Reciting the oath you are no longer me

Then ship off to training with hundreds like you
That also want to sacrifice and to be the few
With basic complete now comes the next step
To train for your job get ready for what's ahead

Graduation has come standing happy and tall
Going before your great nation to serve for them all
They don't understand why you go into fight
Or why you leave home and fly into the night

It's not for the money or even the pride
It's for the freedom we have and the comfort inside
Some will slander and spit call you names
War is not fun war is not a game

(continued on next page)

JUSTIN WIDENER

Protect you and your family from those who want to kill
Our job is keeping you safe with all of our will
Some will come home others will be lost
They gave up their life the ultimate cost

The reasons we serve the reason we sign
Is not to be a hero or anything to hide
We fight for your freedom and carry on our shoulders
To protect all your rights the American soldier

Angels Among Us

Our brothers and our sisters
Some may come by blood
Others created by God
The great and mighty One

They arrive at different times
To help us in our need
They are some human angels
A blessing from God indeed

Guided by our Lord
To do His loving work
Reach out and bless the hearts
Helping those who hurt

You are the given angel
The one I speak about
Sent from the father above
Descended from the clouds

Your kindness is so great
The love you cannot hide
Our prayers that we have prayed
We're humbled deep inside

We thank you for the kindness
That you have shown to us
In our time of need
We're blessed to feel your love

At The Cross

A symbol for the broken a place to find salvation
He died for the world not just one single nation
Not just a piece of wood or a standing decoration
But a place to find redemption with love and adoration

He carried this here cross while mocked and ridiculed
Hated by the people and those who claimed had ruled
He hung there on that cross until his body dead
If only they had listened to the words He said

And when the time had come they lowered His body down
And laid Him in a tomb a distance away from town
A stone to close the tomb the price He surely paid
To take all of our sin and show He is the way

Do not be afraid to come unto the cross
He welcomes all the broken weary and the lost
The ones who hide in sin He holds his arms wide open
Repent of what you've done your life in Him is golden

Come down to the altar and drop on bended knee
Feel the love inside filled with the joy and glee
Don't be nervous or scared let go of all the loss
Take my hand and go and meet me at the cross

PURPOSEFUL POETRY

Blood On The Cross

The cries are heard
Unto your name
Around the world
There is no shame

The voices loud
The prayers come out
We need your love
Is what we shout

In the final hours
Of his life
Jesus cried out
In the dead of the night

If it is your will
Take this from me
Jesus had shouted
With tears on his cheek

The enemy taunted
Laughed and mocked
Jesus that night
His spirit heavily rocked

(continued on next page)

PURPOSEFUL POETRY

He came down from the top
To his eyes did he find
The truth of his followers
Asleep this whole time

The Romans came in force
Search he that is Christ
And Judas would betray
His Lord of that night

Led away in restraints
To die on a tree
So we may live life
Sin we are free

So today we remember
What Jesus did for us
The sacrifices he made
Because we are his love

Come As The Children

Let the little children come
By car or plane or boat
Coming by the millions
To the Lord's Holy throne

Teaching them with love
And building with the strength
Showing them with Jesus
There is no greater gain

Some cultures teach their young
To hate others and to kill
They do not know the Lord
Or live by or father's will

Our children are the future
To walk by foot this land
To reach the list and sick
And be the helping hand

Listen to the words
That Jesus stood and spoke
To every heart that heard
And the dead that he awoke

(continued on next page)

PURPOSEFUL POETRY

You will feel the spirit
Come rushing like a wind
And flooding across the land
Every door it will go in

The lives that will be changed
By those who go before
Will feel the healing power
By Jesus who is Lord

The peace will overwhelm
The power will be great
The love is everlasting
The grace will fill your plate

He replied, "You of little faith, why are you so afraid?" Then he got up and rebuked the winds and the waves, and it was completely calm.
Matthew 8:26

Freedom

My ankles are tied
My wrists are bound
The lack of freedom
To move around

These heavy weights
That hold me down
This negative world
With negative sounds

How do I break
These chains on me
Release my wrists
And set me free

His name is Christ
The One true king
The almighty Savior
To Him we sing

Let go of the past
And live for Him now
He has broken the chains
On our knee we bow

(continued on next page)

PURPOSEFUL POETRY

Do not conform
To this world's lies
To what you will hear
The evil in disguise

Take into the world
And conform to the Lord
Spread of His love
Witnessing more

Live as you teach
By example we will lead
All of God's word
Is what people need

Release all control
You have over life
Believe in our God
And patience for His time

Transform to be used
A seed it will start
And let the Holy Spirit
Overflow in your heart

God Made You

And god sat down and thought one day
To create someone to show the way
Someone who's strong with listening ears
Someone to love beyond the years

Not a giant or a wee little man
But a man who stands on god's own plan
He must be humble and pray from his knees
Like a soldier who goes to where god needs

A smile that glows and shines so bright
A radiance abound with a loving light
Arms so strong that give a hug
To show all others of god's own love

The heart he has will keep the soul
His worth is more than diamonds and gold
With hands so gentle to hold the young
A voice so calm the hymns been sung

And god sat back and said it's good
He makes perfection like no others could
This world will end and god makes new
Until that day god made you

Greater Love

Created with care in the image of you
Lost and broken but still make us new
Continuously sin you do not discard
But always with love you do fill our heart

Mountains will rise and oceans get deep
You will lift us up with no height too steep
More value than gold in your eyes we remain
Undeniable love as you comfort our pain

No storm too strong will ever take
No wind will blow or distance will make
The power of your love within my soul
Your grace and mercy to make me whole

Open the eyes here in my heart
The bond we have never torn apart
We are precious to you never to be sold
More priceless than any diamonds or gold

Until the return of Jesus your Son
When heaven returns and the earth is done
We continue to lift you up in praise
And cherish your love for all of the days

Feed the hungry and locate the lost
We will do our Lord's work at any cost
Faith in our heart and not what we see
Your plans for us are greater than any

Greater Value

Created with care in the image of you
Lost and broken but still make us new
Continuously sin you do not discard
But always with love you do fill our heart

Mountains will rise and oceans get deep
You will lift us up with no height too steep
More value than gold in your eyes we remain
Undeniable love as you comfort our pain

No storm too strong will ever take
No wind will blow or distance will make
The power of your love within my soul
Your grace and mercy to make me whole

Open the eyes here in my heart
The bond we have never torn apart
We are precious to you never to be sold
More priceless than any diamonds or gold

Until the return of Jesus your Son
When heaven returns and the earth is done
We continue to lift you up in praise
And cherish your love for all of the days

Feed the hungry and locate the lost
We will do our Lord's work at any cost
Faith in our heart and not what we see
Your plans for us are greater than any

He Guides My Eyes

The book laid out
Upon the desk
Set to a page
To read no less

The book of Psalms
Contains more word
Written by some men
That needs to be heard

I gaze intently
My eyes aware
I ask the Lord
To start is where

He guides my eyes
And heart to see
The book of Psalms
Chapter seventy-three

The lack of faith
Makes way for pride
The lack of trust
We hold inside

The rich are fat
They take in more
They flash their wealth
And laugh at the poor

The world today
Fits in this word
The rich will flaunt
Turning away from the Lord

I failed to see
What God tells us
Turn our eyes to Him
Feel His love glorious

He said come to me
You that are meek
In my presence you will stand
With my strength no longer weak

Let God be the judge
Lose all of the pride
Fill all of your heart
With love He will provide

(continued on next page)

He Is

He is my strength He is my way
To wake each morning and live another day
He is my joy and loving grace
My rock to stand here in this place

He fills my heart with loving peace
He strengthens my body from my head to my feet
His name is Jesus He is my King
The Prince of peace the love he brings

He has chosen me to be his own
To share his work and what He's sewn
His word is seed to fill the land
His seed will grow by his mighty hand

Where three or more will pray to Him
He will stand with them and fill within
He fills with grace and mercy light
You are not alone He's in your fight

The world is evil and filed with sin
Rejected God and His word within
We have failed and died with many things
With nothing but pride and hate it brings

(continued on next page)

PURPOSEFUL POETRY

Turn back to God the world needs you
Start loving your neighbor and your brother too
Give a smile to others and show there is hope
Start spreading the love and the river will flow

Open up to the many and teach of the peace
And teach from the altar and drop to your knees
Show how to be saved from the sin in your life
For Jesus still lives takes away all the strife

He Strengthens

When I wake up in the morning
To a sun that's shining bright
To the birds that song their song
And the life and guiding light

I do not feel different
But I do feel alone
The problems that I have
The mess I call a home

The bottles sit around
Some empty others full
They are not filled with alcohol
But pills I take in interval

My body is so sick
My strength is always gone
I cannot bend my fingers
My back no longer strong

My heart is pumping hard
My organs run overtime
My system will start failing
This life no longer kind

(continued on next page)

PURPOSEFUL POETRY

I'm walking through this life
The pills become my dope
I need to keep my faith
This Bible is my hope

The world will knock me down
Tell me to give in
Make me feel no worth
Make me feel my sin

I cannot let it win
My Lord is still on high
He strengthens for the battle
He does not pass me by

He died there on that cross
He forgave everyone
His work in us keeps going
The battle will be won

I know there is a purpose
A reason for my life
Cause Jesus is my truth
My path now has a light

His Plan

A fairy tale life with love that has no end
Two little children and a house built with a fence
Princess or a Prince is what you dream of
A wedding in a church with unconditional love

Then one day you awake before your eyes you find
Your life is not that way and dreams are left behind
Your life is full of chaos the walls are coming down
The earth your feet are one is now a shaking ground

A lie is being whispered through your open ear
Your life is not over neither is the end near
In God your life remains and Christ is the start
Quit listening with your mind and listen with your heart

What's broken God will fix He will make it whole
He knows what's in your heart and carry in your soul
Don't question what he's done it is not a mistake
Your partner in this life a bond that He did make

Do not live your life according to all man
Turn your eyes to the king and with you He will stand
Come weather or the winds that want to just destroy
Standing in the Lord you'll live in lasting joy

So dream of what is best and what he wants for you
And pray for one another as they pray for you too
Keep your hope in Christ and build up all the faith
Trusting that His plan will guide you everyday

Hope Lives Here

As the people stand with heads hanging low
Some feel loss and other just don't know
Leaders will come and leaders will leave
Our faith in Jesus will forever cleave

Others have hoped for love and for change
With faith in a world that doesn't know your name
Life speeds right in front as you begin to chase
This world does not care where you stand in this place

Step out of the boundary that man worked to build
But follow the leader with his love you are filled
Open the eyes of your heart not your head
Filling with love to you you are dead

Some made the choice to kill, steal and destroy
They are filled with a hate with no sense of joy
Our God awaits for your choice in this life
A choice with a faith strong like a two edged knife

Build your hope in a Lord and faith with a love
A change to your life sent down from above
Turn away from the evil that roams on the streets
Just follow the Lord and the love that He keeps

Do not become one what the world wants of you
Join in with the millions get out of the pew
Give all of your sins be strong with no fear
Trust in our Lord because hope lives here

How To Love

This day arrives and the sun does shine
What this day holds we soon will find
We feel your love and holy grace
We seek your heart and loving face

We need your comfort here in this place
We trust in you and build our faith
But most all we need your love
What the world provides is not enough

This world destroys and steals away
It turns our hearts from good all day
Give us strength to stand up strong
Knowledge for good and not the wrong

Teach our hearts on how to trust
And not give to the world's lust
We will grow in you you're by our side
Here in this fight I no longer hide

But most of all we ask of you
To change our lives and what we do
Teach us your heart and kingdom above
And how to walk and how to love

I Release You

When you came into this world
A smile came to my face
To hold you tightly in my arms
I felt the power and grace

There is no greater time than this
The love within my heart
This feels just like a fairytale
I promise to do my part

Little hands that were so small
That for so perfect in mine
I'll teach you the ways that you should live
And watch you grow over time

Sadly your time has come to an end
Your fight is now all done
The moments we had and the memories
Each day was filled with fun

I release you now unto the Lord
Into His arms and into His hands
Where you are there is no pain
Or sorrow in the lands

There will be a time when I am called
Into His land I will come
I will never forget who you are
I'll always love you, my son

I Release

The rain falls to the land
The wind is in the air
On this hilltop we stand
Seeing our Lord everywhere

The holy spirit flows
Through our broken hearts
To fill all of those
Who seek a whole new start

We seek to fill our tanks
With everything from you
To you we give our thanks
Your glory following through

The rays of sun will shine
Upon our thirsty souls
Soon our eyes will find
Your loves the greatest goal

You bless us with your grace
And calm us with your mercy
You're loving to our face
And save us when we're hurting

(continued on next page)

PURPOSEFUL POETRY

The chosen road I take
It's riddled with some holes
It is not very straight
Or paved with shiny gold

I cry to you today
To take my little hand
To take on the way
Unto your holy land

My wrongs you will forgive
My sins have been released
The rest of my life I live
In your freedom and your peace

I Stand

A thousand times I've fallen
A million times I've cried
This life has been a struggle
I've felt like I have died

I've bound the evil feelings
That have built up inside
I've spoke your holy name
In fear I continue to hide

The silence is so deafening
This wall that I have built
Surround me and protect me
From the evil I have felt

I seek you for a vision
To fill my empty heart
Help me break down these old walls
And show me where to start

The storm clouds overcome
To keep me from your love
But the sun will break the darkness
With your glory from above

(continued on next page)

PURPOSEFUL POETRY

The people they will talk
And gossip to one another
But the lessons I will learn
As I stand beside my brother

This pain I have inside
Everyday that I will fight
I want to remove the hate
And replace it with your light

The enemy will attack
And come to kill and destroy
But in you I keep my faith
Then my heart will fill with joy

In you I build my trust
To break down all these walls
I lay down all my pride
And listen to your calls

On this mighty day
I stand right by your side
With a faith everlasting
And your love I'll never hide

I Will Give

I'm a senior in high school
Only days until I'm done
I'm unsure of my future
Or what I will become

I don't think I'm ready for college
Or any of the two year schools
I could just get a job as a carpenter
And use my hands to work with tools

My father served in the army
Other family in the Air Force
I could just join a service
But I also wants to play sports

I think I will follow the footsteps
Of those who have gone before
Be a part of a national team
Get to serve the people more

I signed my name on the line
And joined in the military
I handed out a blank check
So people can continue to be free

(continued on next page)

PURPOSEFUL POETRY

The training was tough on me
I pushed myself real hard
But now the training is over
And my new career will start

I serve not for the benefits
Or even the money
I serve for all the people
For their rights and liberty

I put on this uniform
Because I love my country
I lace up these combat boots
To secure that we are free

My family supports my decision
To give of my total life
I hope you will support me too
To protect your family from strife

So when you love your family
And lay your head at night
I vow to all of the Americans
I will fight with all my might

In The Mirror

Cold and wet he sits on the street
With just a jacket and sores on his feet
Asking for change or money they give
This is not the life he wanted to live

Across town sits a single mother
No food to eat or clothes to cover
She drops to her knees tears in her eyes
The child that she holds is her greatest of prize

A little boy hides in a hole in the wall
Afraid of the monster who's scary and tall
Bruises all over with Burns on his arm
Where is the God to keep me from harm

A girl in her teens is forced to do work
To prostitute herself so she doesn't get hurt
Away from her family alone she prays
When will this end and become better days

These are just some of the broken and lost
That Jesus seeks out and his life is the cost
He hears all the prayers that are said in the pain
He hears all the words and they are not said in vain

He sends all his angels he works not alone
You cannot see them they will not be shown
Just look in the mirror and see that it's you
The angel unknown I can help too

It Is Done

The steps He walked across the land
The love that spread by just one man
The lame to walk and blind to see
He came to earth to set men free

He fed the people with His word
Yet faced the lies and felt the sword
With insults hurled the mocking spread
He comforts the living and raises the dead

Instruction He gave to those that follow
Then faced the evil and put it below
Under His foot is where it belongs
The love will prevail and spread with the songs

One night before He sat down to eat
Prayed while He washed and dried each ones' feet
Broke and gave bread and drank in His name
He warned of the hate and betrayal the next day

Tempted and tried while on His knees
You cannot tempt God this we believe
Weeping with tears that fell to the ground
His disciples all sleep and lay one around

(continued on next page)

JUSTIN WIDENER

The soldiers had come to take Him away
In the darkness of night while He kneel and He pray
With swords all extended He is betrayed by a kiss
Arrested on this night in a manner such as this

Bloodied and beaten He's nailed to a cross
The people rejoice not knowing of their loss
As He hangs at the mount tears flow for the Son
Reassures to His mother that now IT IS DONE

Little Hands

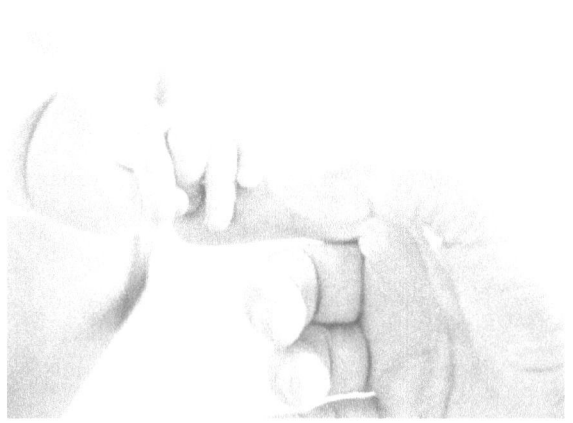

Little hands reach up and hold
A finger with great trust
That finger is connected to
A hand that's filled with love

Those hands have worked real hard
To build, to teach and love each day
Those hands have held some babies
And the hands of others while they pray

Those hands have been burnt and broken
They've felt some awful pain
They've worked and worked each day
For his family's gain

Those hands are not alone in life
They are connected to a man
A man that is happy to hold a hand
Of someone who calls him dad

Muddy Shoes

Muddy shoes so proudly worn
Upon these feet so broken and torn
To walk the roads thus set before
And preach the word of Christ our Lord

The ground is caked upon these souls
It will not stop our greatest goals
To share the word and spread the love
Make sure the spirit flows like a flood

Whether land or sea we need to cross
The wind and waves they will not toss
Just like our Lord we walk the land
Against the evil we take the stand

We find the lost and broken lives
And touch the hearts with prayerful minds
We are agents of hope and transformation
To show the purpose of your salvation

No sin will hold or chain will bind
The mercy and love their hearts will find
The many will listen and seek for more
To change their lives better than before

We need not look to modern man
That state of hope and change their plan
We look to Jesus the only One
Who is the change for all not some

My Son

When you came into this world
A smile came to my face
To hold you tightly in my arms
I felt the power and grace

There is no greater time than this
The love within my heart
This feels just like a fairytale
I promise to do my part

Little hands that were so small
That fit so perfect in mine
I'll teach you the ways that you should live
And watch you grow over time

Sadly your time has come to an end
Your fight is now all done
The moments we had and the memories
Each day was filled with fun

I release you now unto the Lord
Into His arms and hands
Where you are there is no pain
Or sorrow in the lands

There will be a time when I am called
Into His land I'll come
I will never forget who you are
I'll always love you, my son

My Strength

I continue to walk within the trees
When evil attacks I fall to my knees
My Lord appears and takes my hand
He reassures my heart and helps me stand

To follow the path I stand upon
He lifts me up and makes me strong
The love I feel it overflows
He is my refuge this I know

He comforts my heart with every beat
He puts shoes upon these weary feet
No evil can touch or destroy this love
I stand with Christ and His kingdom above

I will climb the mountains that rise up high
Will not look back I have trained my eyes
To look to you my God my Lord
To not give up and follow your word

I surrender to you have no more stress
To strengthen my faith in your righteousness
I open my eyes to your guiding light
And feel your love that's shining bright

Jesus is my rock upon I stand
He will always walk and taking my hand
No thing will stop or make me fear
His kingdom in site with excitement I cheer

No Longer A Number

As I stand and wait for my number to be called
With the evil in this world my life is stalled
The prisoners that live not called by name
Are a pawn to some in this evil game

There is someone who knows your heart
Repent of your sin is where you can start
Just call out his name He does hear your voice
Turn away from this world you make the choice

Some people are offended by certain things
Afraid of the truth and the peace that it brings
Others live in a bubble just fine with their life
Lost in their world and under a knife

Not wanting to step out into the light
Hiding under the covers like a child in the night
So customed to hear their number being called
Not realizing the peace that God has installed

You have a right to the love and the peace
With the love of a God who knows all your needs
Humble your life everyone has a sin
Just knock on His door He will let you in

(continued on next page)

JUSTIN WIDENER

Knock and He will answer seek and you'll find
Ask and receive leave your past in behind
Show mercy to all as He will give you
He loves no one greater but all not a few

As you go forward call out to the Christ
His name is Jesus and He is your light
You're no longer a number he knows of your name
He has your picture on His wall of fame

No Longer One

The snow has fallen and lays upon the ground
Animals hibernating nowhere to be found
With cold in the air everyone in their house
Some are alone as quiet as a mouse

They sit by themselves and stare out the window
They dream of the family and friends that they know
Where are they now you sit and you think
Their fridge has no food no dish in the sink

Reach out to your neighbor extend out your hand
Show them you love and with them you will stand
God did not intend for us to be just one
He wants us together as we are in the Son

He wants us to come to Him as the many
To pray for each other and love company
We are all brothers and sisters in this life
Get down on your knees with others and your wife

As we take the step forward down our road
We walk not alone our Lord bears the load
Just believe in the love and listen to the heart
Walk hand in hand let God do his part

Where two or more have joined He is there too
He hears all your troubles and reaches out to you
Have faith to move mountains to change what you see
Be part of the group it's no longer ME.

Not Finished

WITH EACH DAY WE HOPE TO AWAKE
TO ANOTHER PATH OR JOURNEY WE TAKE
NOT KNOWING THE TROUBLES OR TRIALS THAT ARISE
YOU ARE OUR LORD YOUR LOVE THE PRIZE

WE WORK TO GROW AND BECOME THE BEST
JUST LIKE A SPORT WE'RE PUT TO THE TEST
WE BUILD OUR STRENGTH FOR COMING DAYS
BUT WILL STILL FAIL IN STRUGGLING WAYS

DON'T HANG YOUR HEAD AND FEEL DEFEAT
THE STORMS WILL COME AND WINDS WILL MEET
TO BLOW YOU OFF AND MAKE YOU FALL
BUT LIKE A PASS DON'T DROP THE BALL

THE FIELD IS STACKED THE OPPONENT IS READY
BUT THE LORD WILL GUIDE YOU
AND KEEP YOU STEADY
YOU RUN YOUR JOURNEY TO THE ENDZONE
YOUR GAME ISN'T DONE YOU'RE NOT QUITE HOME

STILL TIME TO PERFECT AND TIME TO GROW
THE PLAYS TO RUN AND ROUTES TO KNOW
LIFE IS LIKE A GAME TO PLAY
WE PRACTICE AND PRACTICE IN EACH DAY

(continued on next page)

PURPOSEFUL POETRY

DO NOT GIVE UP OR GIVE IN TO DEFEAT
THERE IS NO FINISHLINE OR END WE MUST MEET
IN THE LORD WE GROW DO NOT GET UPSET
THE LORD IS STILL WORKING HE'S
NOT FINISHED WITH YOU YET

One Last

It's the sweet-sounding voice of that from your mother
Saying don't be late catch the bus with your brother
The rush of a father giving all a little kiss
An innocent child, thinking of a birthday wish

A police officer working during the morning rush
A little girl in the bathroom just reaching for a brush
There's people all over just living their lives
Sons and daughters husbands and wives

From the north to the south and the east to the west
The people who work to do their best
Anxious to get home and be with the family
To see the smiles and feel the love the only place you want to be

But now in these times of evil and hate
People are living not knowing their fate
A man in a school who fires a gun
A person who decides to kill everyone

The people did not choose to die in this way
They wake up each morning to live another day
A child who was killed and won't be coming home
A mother-of-four who is left all alone

(continued on next page)

PURPOSEFUL POETRY

A baby in a womb who doesn't get to choose
A mother and father whose children will lose
If they only had just one more day
The love they would show or the things they would say

Just one more hug just one more kiss
Just one more smile they don't want to miss
Just one more please and saying thank you
Is enough to change this world's view

When your day is done hurry to your house
Don't be as quiet as a tiny little mouse
Going in through the door with a hi and a hey
Don't worry about tomorrow, just change today

Only If

I wake in the morning and I'm still here
Walk to the bathroom and look in the mirror
The pain I feel the hurt inside
I want to cry and it just hide

The twisting and turning that I still feel
I can't believe this life is real
Lord why do I hurt and why do I cry
I want it to end be with you and the sky

Let me go Lord my story to end
No longer the power to even defend
No one can see as they look into my eyes
I put on a smile and live with the lies

I want someone to listen and not to hear
Who does not get scared and run out of fear
Suicide is an escape and not the right road
I'm tired and weak I can't carry this load

I close myself up away from everyone
I wanted to feel better I want to be done
Lost in this world I feel so alone
I can't wait for the day that you take me home

Until that day comes I will push through
Looking out for others that need help too
Now it's a family right here by my side
I'm glad that I'm here and I haven't died

Our Stand

When we were joined as one
I felt on top of the world
We started our life together
With the three boys and a girl

We've had our times of struggle
But most of all the love
With times of tears and fears
We've turned to a God above

With health that has gotten worse
And stress has become so great
We fight an unseen force
That wants to make us hate

The bills keep coming in
But not enough to even pay
The work exhausts us dearly
Wonder what we'll eat each day

We have fallen in this pit
It feels there's no way out
The further that we go
Have we reached the bottom now

(continued on next page)

JUSTIN WIDENER

The darkness overtakes us
With sadness in the way
We look up to the heavens
And drop to our knees and pray

We're fighting with our faith
The tension that it makes
We open up our ears
To the listening that it takes

We raise our eyes up high
And look for the helping hand
We will fight each day we have
And in Christ we make our stand

Our Time

To live in a day that reminds of past
A time when the world had thrived
A world that grew and loved each other
And people who helped other lives

But times had changed not for the good
The days had become so dark
The walls of peace had fallen down
And evil attacked the heart

What there stood before his eyes
Saddened Nehemiah to a state
A state that brought him to his knees
He pushed away food on his plate

He fasted and prayed for many days
And listened to the Lord
He cried and cried up to the heavens
And waited to hear your word

The generation and world today
Resemble Nehemiah's day
The call goes out to every land
For everyone to pray

(continued on next page)

JUSTIN WIDENER

Do not let the evil to flood
Or destroy your holy home
Your home that beats inside my body
That reassures I'm not alone

We pray and fast here in this day
And ask you to help us fight
The faith we hold and love inside
You are our guiding light

Help us build our homes on rock
And not upon the sand
The waters will rise and winds will blow
With faith and trust this world will always stand

Refill Your Faith Tank

The world will turn
And time continue
The creator is above
With love for you

The reason he created
All that is within
A perfect place to be
Until we welcomed sin

Sin it has created
So many to fall away
The call for no more faith
The name of God don't say

Overcome by all that's bad
With sin sold on the shelf
Our homes being overtaken
Living in a prideful hell

To those who sit and think
While in that church chair
Jesus had called all us
To witness without compare

(continued on next page)

JUSTIN WIDENER

Regain the faith once had
Let truth be heard to all
Stand up in every city
This is an altar call

No longer to be silent
Or speak in voice real low
Get out onto the streets
And let your trumpet blow

The disciples were instructed
To go to all the land
Teach every ear that hear
Raise every willing hand

Refill your heart inside
Your spirit tank of faith
Go out into this world
As our Lord has saith

Let's turn the world around
Back to what our God intends
Filling every heart
With love forever Amen

Save Me A Place In Heaven

The day will come,
When we are all called home
It won't be by a text,
Or a call on the telephone

We do not know the day,
Or even in what hour
The Lord will decide when,
Because it's all in His power

Until the time arrives,
Keep living for the Lord
Do His work here on earth,
And following His word.

To help the little children,
And all of those in need
To grow your faith in God,
And continue to believe

Each day that we live,
Will come and it will pass
So hold onto each moment,
And treat it like the last

(continued on next page)

JUSTIN WIDENER

One day when we awake,
Our loved ones will be gone
The memories we will have,
Of the love and all the fun

But when you are called home,
Your name the angels beckon
My last request to you,
Is save me a place in heaven

Set Free

We walk this earth
A broken ground
A selfish world
With sin all around

The chains attached
To hold us down
We feel defeated
And feel we're drown

The love God has
It is so great
His glorious power
For us to take

He sent his son
To give his life
Forgive our sin
And make things right

He spread his love
To all within
Died on a cross
And rose again

(continued on next page)

JUSTIN WIDENER

He is the key
To all our chains
We are not a number
He knows our names

Stand up and walk
With shackles no more
You are set free
Jesus settled the score

Now open your heart
Unto the ghost
Unto the Lord
Our heavenly host

So spread the word
Of what he's done
Defeated death
The battle was won

Just open your eyes
To this you see
No longer tied down
You are set free

Simple Task

The house of God is where we pray
To bring the tithe and offering today
This path we walk with your guiding love
We set aside our pride your grace is enough

Some will fall and harden their heart
But God never lets go or pulls apart
He guides our hearts outside the walls
Into a land to receive our call

And when we return the site for my eyes
Is one of neglect with no hands to the skies
They've emptied your house and humbled no more
The rooms are all colored and look like a store

I will not let go of what they have done
I will build them up and show you're the One
Turn hearts back to you with heads that will bow
Fight evil with love and sweat from my brow

Lord we ask you to flood all the land
With the spirit inside that comes from your hand
We let go of this world and fall to our knees
From the east to the west your grace and mercy

Each morning you wake the worries aside
He is calling your name no longer you will hide
Every face that you see there He will be
So love one another as you have loved me

Spiritually Dry

Like a leaf that hangs from a tree in the fall
Or the dried out cracks in and old plaster wall
Waiting to be released from the life it once knew
Its life is now over ended all too soon

There are the days that we feel like this leaf
The last one to fall alone from this tree
As we look to our side question to see
Oh Lord our dear Lord just where could you be

We walk down this road and take every step
Feeling scared and alone how far can we get
Which direction to turn which way do I go
Just me in this world out here on my own

Then I hear a song that opens my eyes
To listen to truth and not to the lies
Moisten my heart and water my soul
I ask for your love to make me all whole

I seek for you Lord in a world filled with hate
I feel for you Lord my hand will you take
And then in a moment a whisper in my ear
You tell me Lord Don't worry I am here

With a smile on my face and a warmth in my heart
It strengthens my faith I needed from the start
I thank you Jesus who is the most high
I'm faith filled again no longer spiritually dry

Take The Lead

What is the faith or to keep the hope
Will you continue fall or hold onto the rope
Where is the trust not in yourself
But a God who loves and is there to help

In today's world the love of ones own
Will you live for yourself and reap what you've sewn
Here in this day which way will you turn
Your life you will lose or bridge that you burn

Live dead to yourself and all that you have
Find hope in the Lord right now while you can
The battle will rage for your life for your soul
Evil will destroy but Jesus wants you whole

Where are all his children with arms all raised
The ones who stand up in them He is praised
Every corner of this earth on sea and on land
The lost we will find put food in their hand

The bombs that explode leave bodies that are dead
The hate that is seen the death that is spread
Help God change the hearts of those who are lost
Live dead to yourself and give any cost

The Lord will call you to stand on the line
Your name will be called now is your time
It is all a mission to help those in need
Do not be a follower stand up take the lead

The Day

The day will come when I leave this place
And I stand before you face-to-face
What will I say or what will I do
The old is gone I have become new

Well I touch your hands and see the holes
Drop to my knees wash your feet and soles
I may have died but now I live
My sins are gone and I forgive

That day will come I hold your hand
You take me before the Creator to stand
My eyes will see your radiant light
No darkness near for all is bright

That day when I will kiss your face
To see your kingdom with every race
Every tribe and tongue and nation will stand
Together in love across your land

That day will come when I hear my name
Called by my Lord in Paradise I gain
Well done my good and faithful servant
Your sins are gone because you repent

(continued on next page)

PURPOSEFUL POETRY

That day will come when I'm welcomed home
And see my life as I was never alone
He walked beside me all of my days
He loved me and held me with all of his grace

That day will come when we all get to see
The truth is revealed with all his Mercy
That day will come when fear is no more
The only emotion is the love all galore

The Final Teardrop Fallen

The final teardrop fallen
Upon the dusty ground
The soldiers filled with fright
Looking all around

They knew what had happened
The man upon this cross
Was just as he had stated
This was the Son of God

The damage that had followed
The carnage that they find
Was nothing ever seen
Or known of any kind

The spirit of the Son
Was taken into hell
For all of the mankind
For sin to be dispelled

Mother Mary filled with sorrow
Her Son hanging on this cross
Knowing that He is the chosen
Son of almighty God

(continued on next page)

PURPOSEFUL POETRY

His body laid to rest
Enclosed inside a tomb
His disciples filled with fear
And locked inside a room

As the third day came
The stone was rolled away
Jesus rose and walked
With nothing in His way

The resurrection filled
There is no longer death
He is risen to the highest
And become the living breathe

The Focus

With eyes that wander and move around
The streets I walk throughout this town
The signs I see that cross my path
These clothes I wear are all I have

The shoes I wear upon my feet
Are torn and worn not very neat
No place to lay no comfy bed
The ground is where I lay my head

I walk in fear each day I live
I look for help nowhere will give
I'm scared of evil around every turn
I hear the lies and feel the burn

So much hate out on the street
No place to even escape the heat
I look for food in garbage cans
The germs that live on dirty hands

Can't sleep at night I have this fear
The devil will kill me while I am here
But then one day I heard this voice
It said don't worry you have a choice

(continued on next page)

PURPOSEFUL POETRY

A choice to focus on all the bad
Or remember the times that made me sad
Also a choice to go and hear his word
A place that is safe I will not be hurt

I chose the road of faith and trust
The narrow path is now a must
I know he walks right by my side
I profess my love no longer hide

I once was afraid the devil was there
Afraid he was hiding everywhere
But the Lord spoke loudly and then I knew
He is with me and everywhere too

The Gift Of Life

The gift of life
Is given each day
I choose to live
Not by my way

I raise my eyes
Up to the sky
But the enemy continues
With all his lies

I will not listen
To what he said
My Lord is alive
He is not dead

I will pray all day
To my God above
And trust His ways
Are filled with love

The enemy will try
To intimidate me
To destroy my hope
And all I believe

(continued on next page)

PURPOSEFUL POETRY

This body I have
Will become weak
The enemy tells me
I am but meek

But my God will strengthen
Stand me up on my feet
And show me the path
As he walks next to me

In Him I have love
Abundant joy and hope
I no longer will fear
But keep eyes on my home

The Mission

We're born into this world to love one another
We're raised by our father and by our mother
Taught the way to live and go out to the others
Work, live and love to all my sisters and brothers

What is my mission the reason for my life
To just have a home some children and a wife
What will it do for me to help the meek and sick
To give them my last dollar what will they do with it

My mission is to help to witness and to preach
To go unto the village and all the people teach
To show them his great love the will he has for all
I will serve my mighty Lord I answer to the call

There's never just one mouth needed to be fed
Rescue all the sinners Jesus' mission will be met
We walk this dusty land through the snow and rain
To spread His holy word to heal those with pain

Our mission is your kingdom your presence in all life
We walk the rocky path through day and all the night
You are our light that shines on the path we walk
For us defeated death no longer on that cross

The Power

The word of God has power
To strengthen and heal and raise
Spoken to the people
To follow all of these days

It will break down the walls
Bring together all the lands
Showing nothing but one color
Filling hands with other hands

Reaching out to all the towns
Opening every heart
Fill them with the light
Is where we need to start

We no longer are a slave
To the evil worldly ways
We will rejoice in Him
From now and the coming days

Bring all of those who've sinned
Who've turned straight from the Lord
And break the chains of pattern
Let's spread His living word

Put your words here in my mouth
And your love fill up my heart
I will walk the road before me
By my side you never part

The Reason

The stars hang high with snow on the ground
Christmas cheer is spread all around
Decorations galore fill windows this season
The people lose sight of the true reason

A man in red in a chair at the mall
With children that visit wishes big wishes small
People crowd the stores buying everything in sight
And try to get finished before it is night

The story first began over 2000 years ago
A baby was born that the world will soon know
A king born for all a priest born to teach
He walked many miles for the people he would reach

(continued on next page)

PURPOSEFUL POETRY

The blind He gave sight the deaf would now hear
He came to the lands His followers then to cheer
He raised from the dead a man with his word
The lame would too walk His voice that they heard

He warned of the temple rebuilt in three days
The pharaoh had feared the change of the ways
Sent out a pastor to challenge this man
Find fault in His word tear down his stand

He taught all the men and women of that day
Of what God expected the path and the way
Guiding the souls finding all those who are lost
He gave of Himself not sparing a cost

His time here on earth an end to His life
He stood there on trial and suffered the strife
Unto the Creator He did soon arise
He is the only Son His name Jesus Christ

The Resurrection

When I fall
You lift me up
When I thirst
I drink from your cup

When I am lost
You take my hand
When I am weak
Your strength I stand

You gave your life
For my sins
Your blood runs deep
With mighty winds

The cross you bear
Was tall and strong
Your body lay dead
Not very long

Wrapped in a sheet
Laid in a grave
The third day came
The stone rolled away

(continued on next page)

PURPOSEFUL POETRY

Into the light
You came with peace
Your followers saw
But Thomas not believe

Look into my hands
You see the hole
Teach what you see
So the world will know

I did defeat
Death is no more
Your sins are forgiven
The stripes I wore

Now from this time
Go out and teach
My father's word
For you to preach

Demonstrate the love
I have shown you
Into this world
The many and few

I ascend to the kingdom
My father's land
Seated at the throne
At his right hand

(continued on next page)

JUSTIN WIDENER

The day will come
When you are called
Leave the world behind
A new life to behold

Accept my love
My body striped
The only way
The truth and the life

I go before
To prepare a place
Just follow my word
And trust in my ways

The Rocks

The waves will flow and beat the shore
Changing the rocks different from before
They open the holes that no longer hide
Open to the world the rocks collide

The Lord will fill your emptiness
His hand is strong when you feel helpless
The Lord exclaimed to all the men
When this life ends your new one begins

Find the path He wants you on
Be patient and listen with him you are strong
Help those you see who struggle along
This journey you follow is very long

But while you are here living on this land
Preach of His word and make that stand
Be born again not from the womb
But by the water and the spirit too

You will be mocked and treated wrong
Believe in Him you are that strong
When the end comes and this world fails
You stand in His presence and love you will hail

The Saviour

With snow on the ground a chill in the air
The time has arrived with the lights everywhere
Some feel all offended change the name of the season
Have lost all the faith to know Jesus is the reason

Jesus came here but to love not to hate
Break the chain of the sin that kept you from his gate
He humbled himself to show how to live
Taught many of masses not to take but to give

This baby that is born is great and a king
The choir of the angels in the heavens will all sing
The heavens have opened letting out guiding light
With a star in the sky shining bright in the night

(continued on next page)

PURPOSEFUL POETRY

Emmanuel He is called meaning God is with us
Bringing hope to the many in Him you can trust
Called by your name to love one another
No one is a stranger we're all sisters and brothers

The people that you see who have less than you
They are loved by our Lord just the same He loves you
When you see them around extend out a hand
Show them Christ's love and help them to stand

Go forward in this day you do not walk alone
He guides you on the path the path to our home
With love in your heart and eyes not on fame
Walk always in faith Jesus is his name

The Seed

The seed that falls falls by the side
No sun to touch just a rock to hide
The clouds move in and the rain does fall
The seed is moved to begin its call

God puts it where He wants it to be
The place to grow for many to see
If it does not die it not will grow
Or spread the love for all to know

You are the seed in God's great land
He does not leave you He is your hands
Live dead to yourself not for your own
And live for all others your seed to be sewn

Touch ever nation all undiscovered lands
To spread the word for Christ you will stand
Let your fruit be plenty and grow for your brother
Fill all of their bellies with love like a mother

Stand up from your chair take hold of the reigns
We are not a number the Lord knows our names
Put forth the first step the others will follow
Take your brother's hand and bring them to our home

(continued on next page)

PURPOSEFUL POETRY

Our home in the kingdom that is waiting for you
Your mansion is built and peace is the truth
Christ died for our sin hung up on the cross
He paid all our debt His life was the cost

When a child looks your way look into their eyes
Their heart is innocent they know not the lies
Protect them from evil he wants to destroy
Put Christ in your heart and be filled with the joy

The Walls

The walls will stand
That were built by hand
Your word is read and
Your love upon the land

The joy released to each of all
Our hearts within have felt the call
Unto our God with open ears
The path to take for coming years

We feel the power and loving grace
Let the rain fall down upon our face
Going to the lost to make them found
Miss not one corner or unturned ground

Tithing first of fruits is our father's law
Have faith in our God the closer we draw
And honor the Sabbath that we must rest
To do His work and give of our best

The walls we build will fill with joy
Inside our hearts the spirit enjoy
We walk the world to spread the love
With peace and grace down like a dove

The Way

The lessons learned
The word was spoke
He told the many
Of those who oppose

He did not teach
To fight in return
He taught to love
And help them learn

You will be hated
By the non-believers
Preach my words
And make them achievers

You will not charge
A shekel or coin
The love is free
For all to join

I extend my mercy
And loving grace
To all that follow
And turn their face

(continued on next page)

JUSTIN WIDENER

Everything you have
Is yours on loan
It belongs to God
You are his own

Give unto God
That belongs to him
Have faith in the Lord
With love within

Walk into the world
Outside the church doors
And take to the streets
Bring more to the Lord

The day is coming
Of the Lord's return
Save your brothers and sisters
From hell's eternal burn

Take a minute out of life
Or take all of your day
Extend a helping hand
To show others the way

These Chains

My ankles are tied
My wrists are bound
The lack of freedom
To move around

These heavy weights
That hold me down
This negative world
With negative sounds

How do I break
These chains on me
Release my wrists
And set me free

His name is Christ
The One true king
The almighty Savior
To Him we sing

Let go of the past
And live for Him now
He has broken the chains
On our knee we bow

(continued on next page)

JUSTIN WIDENER

Do not conform
To this world's lies
To what you will hear
The evil in disguise

Take into the world
And conform to the Lord
Spread of His love
Witnessing more

Live as you teach
By example we will lead
All of God's word
Is what people need

Release all control
You have over life
Believe in our God
And patience for His time

Transform to be used
A seed it will start
And let the Holy Spirit
Overflow in your heart

This Is

Snowflakes falling on the rooftop
Glistening in the winter sun
Snowflakes falling all around us
Makes for a lot of winter fun

Children laughing as their playing
Sledding down the snow filled hills
A gentle wind blowing on them
Makes for a brisk winter chill

Mothers standing in their doorways
With smiles upon their faces
The joy they have in their children
Running through the open spaces

This is winter time
The time to spread the love and joy
This is Christmas time
The time for every girl and boy

The time to sing
The bells to ring
Trees go up
With Christmas stuff

(continued on next page)

JUSTIN WIDENER

This is Christmas
The time to remember
What he gave to us
His life to surrender

The church on the corner
Has a manger that sits near
A scene we all love to
See this time of year

Everyone celebrates
The joy and the reason
The baby who's birth is
The time for the season

Jesus born to the world
His life is for all
He gave to the many
He answered the call

This Christmas remember
To spread the holiday cheer
To everyone around you
To those far and near

This Road

This road is full of bumps
A lot of crazy turns
With each step I walk or run
There's lesson to be learned

The world is full of sadness
The tears continue to flow
The evil in the hearts
Will continue to grow and grow

No king that walks this land
Can help or remove the pain
Only God can help his people
And His love is not in vain

The power of his promises
The blessings all poured out
The spirit He provides
The world will want to shout

He expects us to show love
As He has done for us
To help our brothers and sisters
Giving food and water a must

(continued on next page)

JUSTIN WIDENER

To teach and preach of Jesus
No evil will be said
With Jesus there is a life
With evil you're just dead

God will provide abundance
Have faith and trust in Him
Jesus' arms will be our safety
No evil will come within

Take up your armor of God
Your sword and helmet and shield
Preparing for the fight
This world, it will not yield

Go back on to your father's land
The place of ruin and dust
Proclaiming the word of God
With power in your bust

The serpent will be crawling
And destroying up ahead
But with the faith of Jesus
Your boot will stomp his head

This Rusty Ol' Pot

Outside in the rain or a kitchen of a home
The color that it shows is a message of its own
It's been used as a drum or to cover a head
It's been used on the stove so many are fed

Others you will find in a shiny and clean way
Hung from a rack in a work of display
Kept clean in a kitchen for others to view
It sparkles and shines just like it is new

But this rusty old pot is used as a step
For children of all ages to reach and to get
To put out a fire or fill a children's pool
It is not just an item it is a rusty old tool

It feeds all the poor not just Kings and the Queens
A husband and wife with their children and teens
This rusty old pot has a story if it's own
A story for the ages the generations that have grown

It may not look pretty or catch someone's eye
But it's been there for us as the years have passed by
There will be a time when its day comes to an end
It may have a hole or the handles start to bend

(continued on next page)

JUSTIN WIDENER

But I am this pot all dirty and used
Faithful to many even though was abused
No matter my looks I still have a purpose
To help those I can and to calm those who are nervous

Until the day comes that my God takes me home
I will continue this path I know not alone
Just like the pot still works in my worst
Just remember the word the last will be first

Until We Meet Again

We shared the same blood
But still you were my friend
Separated by the miles
But connected until the end

Our age was only months
Our likes were not the same
We were different on the outside
And different in our name

With God guiding our paths
And holding our every tear
We were sure to grow apart
Yet together every year

The road became so rough
And bumpy for this ride
The twists and turns before us
The world's not on our side

Then one day it came
The call to change everything
The call that you were gone
The pain that it did bring

(continued on next page)

JUSTIN WIDENER

Taken from this world
Too early in this life
The loving heart we knew
It doesn't feel right

The tears are dried and gone
Our hearts have come to mend
With families of our own
We love without an end

We know that you are safe
In heaven with our Prince
We never said goodbye
Only until we meet again

Unto The World

THE BOAT IS TIED
UNTO THE DOCK
THE MEN WHO BOARD
WILL BE A FLOCK

THIS MAN WALKED UP
TO THOSE FROM BEHIND
THEY DROPPED THEIR NETS
TO LOVE ALL KIND

HE CALLS THEM DISCIPLES
FOLLOWERS OF THE LORD
HE TOLD THEM TO TEACH
AND PREACH TO THE WORLD

GO OUT TO THE MANY
FORM NOT JUST A BOND
TO BUILD A RELATIONSHIP
WITH LOVE THAT IS STRONG

INVEST NOT WITH MONEY
WITH PAPER COLORED GREEN
BUT INVEST IN THE HEART
AND SPIRIT HOLY

(continued on next page)

JUSTIN WIDENER

SO GO INTO THE WORLD
OUT ONTO THE STREET
WITH ARMS HELD OPEN
AND LOVE YOU WILL GREET

JUST FOLLOW THE PATH
THE LORD SET BEFORE
THOSE WHO ARE LOST
NEED LOVE EVEN MORE

AS YOU TRAVEL THE LAND
NO BRIDGE WILL BE BURNED
TOUCH EVERYONE'S HEART
NO STONE GOES UNTURNED

We Drop To Our Knees

The night would come
Of Jesus' last
The supper he ate
The word was cast

He prayed alone
For what's to come
Tears flowing down
For everyone

Then Judas had led
The law to him
Betrayed with a kiss
A man with no sin

Whipped and beaten
Accused of a lie
He spread the truth
They wanted him to die

The sin of all
Taken by this man
He rose again
In all God's plan

(continued on next page)

JUSTIN WIDENER

Defeated death
Forgave all sin
Relieved the weight
For man to come in

The kingdom of God
Given to you
His perfect land
From a nail in a hand

We drop to our knees
Before your throne
You lift up our heads
And call us your own

We are now home
This is the place
No longer alone
In God's saving grace

We Will Stand

Questions they arise
Throughout the land
We work and slave
No more we stand

Why should we live
Under other's rule
We give ourselves
Are we the fool

Through our brother now
We hear you Lord
The way we acted
Not served before

We stand together
And stand as one
The fight we'll fight
The victory is won

Our faith in the Lord
We may still fall
We will rise again
When we hear the call

The path is paved
Set right before
To the land that's given
From our great Lord

Will You?

The looks you get when you lift your hand
The comments made when you take a stand
This is just normal for some don't know
They wander the world which direction to go

Living in fear loving only one's self
Leaving faith to get dusty like a book on a shelf
Shedding some tears crying in pain
No matter how far the faith will remain

You choose only to believe the world and it's lies
The fortune being told see only with your eyes
Now open your eyes the ones with your heart
Feeling love in your body let Him do His part

Your name will be called from the tops of the hills
Trust in His plan and all the He wills
You should not fight or even protest
Stand strong in your life and yell out a yes

Jesus was born left heaven to be man
To show and to teach all that we can
With God you can trust in Him and His plan
Your are child of the great and mighty I Am.

As you go forward and walk in this world
Have faith like Mary a young virgin girl
Follow His plan and listen to His word
As for you and your house will you serve the Lord

Without A God

The seed is sewn
Into the ground
Watered daily
With sun abound

And when it grows
A harvest reap
Our God commands
A tenth He keep

Sometimes the seed
Will grow astray
Shaded from sun
And light of day

The day may come
It turns its faith
To not believe
And look away

No longer believe
In God above
The seed proclaims
With no love

(continued on next page)

JUSTIN WIDENER

Truth does exist
In plain site
The words proclaim
With God's almight

Without a God
There'd be no love
Without a God
To reign above

The truth appears
Before our eyes
The truth exists
Much more than lies

Faith will rise
And grow good seed
With Jesus Christ
To shine indeed

The Lord is truth
He is the life
Water your seed
It will come alive

You Are

The calendar changes a new year to start
The past is behind new beginning for your heart
With eyes lifted high I look to your will
Your mercy will guide your grace my life fill

In this walk that we take the steps where they fall
We listen to your voice our names to the call
My spirit to empower with strength from above
The power that you hold come down like a dove

Obedient to your will life based off of the word
Open up to the lost speak your love to be heard
Release all the flesh live not just in man
Be washed in the faith beside you He will stand

Give not to the tempting ways of the world
The seduction of man the sins that are hurled
For the enemy comes to kill steal and destroy
He ruins the lives of all seeking joy

As it shows in Ezekiel speaking to the dry bones
Following our God and the Spirit fill your own
Let's throw out the garbage get rid of the waste
The divine in your mouth and the peace you will taste

The dark cannot stand when you are in the light
His image in us all in you He shines bright
Sit down to His word and open your eyes
Be open to the truth forget all the lies

You Don't Have Me

One day I wake and open my eyes
Look at the sun as it starts to rise
I step out of bed with a problem to stand
I reach for my glasses as they fall from my hand

Shaking my head and trying to see
What is this feeling thats happening to me
I cough and I gasp as I'm trying to breathe
I just don't feel right I'm sick I believe

Go to the doctor the blood tests are done
The MRI test is never any fun
I sit and I wait for the doctor to come in
The knock on the door as he enters again

A somber looking face takes a seat in the chair
I'm scared into tears this pain that I bear
He comforts me with a nurse in the room
He gives me the news my life will end soon

By now I am bawling my eyes are all filled
I think of the many that cancer has killed
My way home I stop I pray and I cuss
I thought you were with me protecting all of us

(continued on next page)

PURPOSEFUL POETRY

I gather myself and arrive to my home
I tell all my family as I shake on the phone
This Sunday in church I question my faith
I ask you for strength that I need in these days

As I kneel at the altar you speak in my ear
And tell me to come and give all my fear
You give me the comfort when I feel alone
Now is not the time that I'll be called home

With this new strength and journey ahead
With the power of the Lord the cancer is dead
I stand in my faith and trust and believe
I have this cancer YOU DON'T HAVE ME

Your Name

As I stand and wait for my number to be called
With the evil in this world my life is now stalled
The prisoners that live not called by their name
Are a pawn to some in this evil game

There is someone who knows your heart
Repenting of your sin is where you can start
Just call out his name He does hear your voice
Turn away from this world you make the choice

Some people are offended by certain things
Afraid of the truth and the peace that it brings
Others live in a bubble just fine with their life
Lost in their world and under a knife

Not wanting to step out into the light
Hiding under the covers like a child in the night
So customed to hear their number being called
Not realizing the peace that God has installed

You have a right to the love and the peace
With the love of a God who knows all your needs
Humble your life everyone has a sin
Just knock on His door He will let you in

(continued on next page)

PURPOSEFUL POETRY

Knock and He will answer seek and you'll find
Ask and receive leave your past in behind
Show mercy to all as He will give you
He loves no one greater but all not a few

As you go forward call out to the Christ
His name is Jesus and He is your light
You're no longer a number he knows of your name
He has your picture on His wall of fame

My Child

Before you were formed
I knew you
Sculpted with love
And a heart that is true

I created the plan
I have for your life
But evil has invaded
In the form of a knife

The tears from the babies
Caused by abortion
Are enough to fill up
Even the largest ocean

Sister or mother
A father or brother too
You will never know
The joy I have for you

Man has stolen the pen
I use to write your page
Evil has stolen the hearts
Of people of every age

(continued on next page)

PURPOSEFUL POETRY

Just know you have a place
In my kingdom up above
With a peace you've never known
Every day is filled with love

From the day you were conceived
To the beat of your little heart
Growing in your mother
Then the doctor tore you apart

I have been right by your side
And held your little hand
My child you are a treasure
A grand part of my plan

For future generations
My children will still fight
To battle evil people
And spread to those my light

There will become a time
When this evil world will end
Believe me when I say
You will love my plan again

www.ingramcontent.com/pod-product-compliance
Lightning Source LLC
Chambersburg PA
CBHW021428070526
44577CB00001B/120